SCRIBBLES

AKSHIKA SINGH

Copyright © Akshika Singh
All Rights Reserved.

To my mom and dad

Contents

1. My School

During this lockdown, I miss my school
Along with all of its rules.
Walking with hands behind back
Seeing shelves with books stacked
I miss the students' laugh
And all the members of the staff
The children making noise
The teachers standing with poise
I miss playing handball.
Though while playing sometimes fall.
Blowing in the field, the cool pleasant breeze.
Which would blow down leaves from tall, shady trees
I wish that the pandemic ends and school reopens again
So, I can go back without fear of getting the Covid pain.

2. Panipat – The Great Betrayal

One cool breezy eve

I decided to leave.

To see a movie

Based on history

The movie was Panipat's third battle

The clash of swords made my bones rattle

The scenes of blood

And splatters of mud

Made my courage shut

Like a flower's bud

I saw a back, that was stabbed

By someone whose empathy was what he lacked

The Marathas fell back one by one.

As they fought while their backs were turned

Because the alliance was filled with traitors.

More than one

That is why the Afghans were the ones who won.

But this wasn't the end of the story,

As the Marathas still wanted their glory

They wanted to take back what they lost

As they didn't want to be remembered as the ones who lost

The Afghans died one by one

And the Marathas knew that this time they had won.

3. The Boy Who Hated History

There was a boy who hated history
He used to think it was an impossible mystery
Leonardo's painting, the Mona Lisa
The Egyptian Pyramids of Giza
In his history examination syllabus
Was the civilization on the river Indus
Memorising answers that were huge
Made his brain totally confused
He tried to study for a while
Mona Lisa's legendary smile
After some time, he felt so bored that
He fell asleep at his desk and snored.

4. CORONA VIRUS

C is for the Chaos you have caused

O is for the flight Operations you have paused

R is for the Roar of sadness people make

O is for no Options left to take

N is for the New normal of being locked in our homes.

A is for Anxiety spread across the world like a dome.

V is for the Vaccine soon to be created

I is for Isolation no longer needed.

R is for people dancing in the Rain

U is for Us meeting each other again

S is for now Staying home and staying safe.

5. Soft People Are Stronger

Though you wouldn't understand
That every harsh word of yours
Hurts us the most; as we believe you
To be as good to us as we are to you
Every insult, every taunt
It may be said for fun and it may not
But whatever the case, you must know
That it causes us unbearable pain
You know us as soft- the ones who always cry
But crying is a way to express pain
When words have stranded us
on a dismal island
We are the soft ones
The most empathetic of the lot
Disregarding ourselves for others,
knowing that if we take time for ourselves alone
All you would say is
They're so selfish, they cry all the time
To earn sympathy by creating drama
And never care about the people around"
None of you can ever understand
The pain that comes with being sensitive
We're made fun of all the time
For trying to make others feel better

And then if we don't, we
"Only care about ourselves, crying all the time"
We cry we weep yes, it's true
But most importantly we do so because of you
You don't try understanding us
And always expect us to be empathetic
We do like affection in large amounts
And you could say that you don't, we would listen
But no, you wouldn't
As you love having excuses to be mad at us
Yelling at us for being "clingy"
But what else can we do
To show that we may be different but are humans just like you
What else shall we need to do
For you to respect and accept us the way we are
And we know simple words will not change your mind
But always remember soft people are stronger
Way more than you could ever be.

6. Devotee of the Moon

Lurking amongst the shadows
Look up to the waxing moon
And howl your melancholy call
That echoes around the forest
Announcing the presence
Of the king of the dark
The ground trembles at your feet
Recognizing its true lord
Summon your followers
The ones you protect
The warriors of the pack
Defending your domain
Under your authority
Your boldness unmatched
Air ruffling your fur
Those clever amber eyes
Instilling fear within intruders
The epitome of wisdom
Being reliable and strong
The Alpha committed to the night
And pledged for eternity to your pack

7. The Dark

Isn't the white piece of paper useless
Without the dark smudge of ink?
Aren't ravens called the smartest
Isn't the very road you walk on
Amongst every other bird?
Dyed black by tar?
Isn't it also a symbol?
That light will be there soon?
Doesn't it wait until the light reaches?
The brightness of dawn
Following the dark hours of night.
When light was created,
You didn't banish the dark,
It exists, still, in the curls of your hair,
In your shadows, one of the few
Companions that never leave.
Pondered I, looking over the asleep world
Hoping for someone who agrees with me
As even for the moon it's exhausting

8. Warrior

She was not fragile like a leaf
That she would crumple.
She was fragile like glass
Break her and you would bleed
For she had been forged in the flames of despair
With the power of the sky in her veins
And the rage of the sea in her soul
She pulled herself up, yet again
From the pit, she had slipped into,
Willing to fight again.
Her resistance was unnerving
For the monstrosity that beheld her.
Defiant, as her wounds healed,
Defiant, as she wiped the blood from her face;
She looked into his eyes
Her message was clear
That she would never back down.
Every time he tried breaking her,
She would come back stronger
For she wasn't an ordinary warrior,
She was the greatest of them all
She was Hope.
Tired of people around her
Memories of each day seem a blur

She makes a decision: she's had enough of the pain
Had enough of her self-esteem broken part by part
Just before time stops her heart,
Her last wish remains;
To be praised for what she did
And not again be compared to another kid
Her friend, whose tears are to the brim
Somehow enduring life
Though the people around him
Are worse than a poisoned knife.

www.ingramcontent.com/pod-product-compliance
Lightning Source LLC
Chambersburg PA
CBHW021202130726
47988CB00004B/1726